Bushcraft Survival Skills for Beginners: Master The Bushcraft Basics - Fundamentals, Tools & Safety, & Self-Sufficiency For Your First Time Journey

Andy Ferguson

© 2015

Disclaimer

Table of Contents

Introduction

The word 'Bushcraft' is one that gets thrown around enough to the point that we have a general idea of what it means when we hear it, but we might not be able to come up with a specific definition. Bushcraft is simply defined as the skills that are needed to live or survive out in the bush, or the wilderness.

But learning Bushcraft skills doesn't just teach us what we need to know to get out of a survival situation we may find ourselves in. It teaches us to thrive in it. That means learning how to live off the land by giving yourself warmth and security in the form of fire and shelter, sustaining yourself by hunting, fishing, and foraging, carving your own tools out of wood and other natural materials, and any other necessities for living comfortably in the wilds.

As you are new to the subject of Bushcraft, this book is here to teach you all of the fundamentals that you need to know. That means diving into the definition of Bushcraft with much more detail, learning critical outdoor survival skills, the core tools that are needed for Bushcraft survival and how you can build/acquire them, tips for becoming totally self-sufficient in the wild, and then instructions for Bushcraft projects that you can use to begin your journey.

Far too few people know the skills to make it out of a survival situation alive, let alone to actually thrive off of the land on their own and be totally self-sufficient in it. Is this book here to teach you how you can become a professional Bushcraft survival expert? No. But what you will learn in this book is the fundamentals that will stick with you for the rest of your life if you ever plan on becoming one. So turn the page and begin the learning process, and soon enough, you'll be converting the knowledge you learn in this book into skills.

Stay tuned...

Chapter 1: What is Bushcraft?

We have just defined 'Bushcraft' as the skills that are needed to not only survive out in the woods, but to thrive in it. Let's explore that definition with more depth here in this chapter.

People in general are becoming far too dependent on the modern lifestyle that we have become accustomed to thanks to the rapid advancement of technology. As little as ten years ago, would you have known that everyone living today wouldn't go from one corner of the house to the other without taking a mobile or electronic device with them? Twenty years ago, would it have been thought possible that the internet would have become just as necessary as water or electricity? Regardless of what your answers are, the point is that humanity in general has drifted farther apart from nature than it ever has before.

The ancestors of every person today had an extensive knowledge of bushcraft skills because they had an absolute necessity to survive in the wilderness. To do so, they needed to become one with the wilderness, but making a connection with nature and using only what was needed to survive.

Are there people who have these kinds of skills today? Yes there are, but they are few and far and in between. The few professional bushcraft experts that you know of are likely the ones that you have seen on Reality TV. All in all, mankind has become so far disconnected from nature that if the grid were to go down tomorrow and everyone was thrown back into the Stone Age, so few people would be prepared to live without the special amenities that they are used to. You don't have to be one of these people.

Bushcraft promotes healthy knowledge, physical exercise, and activities that are both friendly to the environment and allow one to sustain themselves. You can have all of the survival gear and knowledge in the world, but still feel uncomfortable while out in the woods with a simple goal of wanting to get out as fast as you can. For the professional bushcraft expert, the wilderness would feel like home and they couldn't be any more comfortable surviving in it.

Learning to use bushcraft skills will dramatically enhance both your physical and emotional well being. The connection that you will feel with nature is simply incomparable to any connection you may feel with modern life. Bushcraft skills will take some time and trial and error processes to master, but each and every one of them can be learned by the individual who puts the effort into it.

The primary bushcraft skills that you must learn are the following:

- Making a Home – building a workable overnight shelter is one thing, but building a stronger and larger shelter where you could live for weeks if not months is a whole other ball game. You don't have conveniences such as the grocery store around the corner or the internet or electricity, but what you do have is abundant natural resources at your disposal to build a shelter and a fire to give you warmth and security.

- Food and Water - like we have just mentioned, you won't have the grocery store around the corner you can travel to. But you still have abundant natural resources in front of you. By using skills in bushcraft, you must learn to hunt, trap, fish, forage, and cultivate. Not only must you learn to gather food resources in this manner, but you have to learn how to cook, prepare, and preserve them as well. The same goes for water; even if you gather multiple gallons worth of water, if your water is left out in the heat it goes bad pretty quick and then drinking it would be more risky than not drinking any water at all! You have to learn what water sources are safer and which ones to avoid, and then how to filter, purify, and store it.

- Tools - by living for a time in the wilderness, you'll be able to take some tools you can pick up at the sporting goods or army navy store with you. But there are still many tools that you will have to make on your own as you set up your way of life.

- Medical – this one is huge. Accidents can and will happen out in the wilderness, and even the smallest of cuts can develop into a dire infection that puts your entire wilderness experience on the ropes. Fortunately, nature has an abundance of natural remedies just waiting to be used. Having the knowledge to take advantage of those things could be a life saver if and when the time comes.

The point of this chapter is to teach you that by using bushcraft skills, it's just you and the wilderness. You might be with someone else, but for the most part, you must learn on your own to become a part of the nature cycle rather than try to fight it, which would be the instinct of many people who find themselves lost or attempt to survive out in the wilds.

However, when you first walk into the wilderness you are nowhere near the top of the totem pole. Nature already has a giant leap ahead of you, but by learning survival knowledge and turning it into skills, you can definitively work your way up. In the process, you'll learn to enjoy the wilderness, not to feel disheartened by it.

Chapter 2: Fundamental Bushcraft Skills

The topic of this chapter really could be expanded into an entire book, as there is nearly a limitless amount of knowledge that you could learn about outdoor survival skills. With that in mind, we will just cover the basics of the most fundamental bushcraft skills that must stick with you for the rest of your life.

The first most important skill to have in bushcraft is a survival mentality. Your mentality will determine your attitude, which in turn will determine how successfully you will be in a survival situation. When developing a survival mentality, always remain focused on the fact that you can survive for about three minutes without air, three hours with regulating your body temperature, three days without water (although you feel the negative effects of dehydration in less than one) and three weeks without food. The point of this is to teach you what comes as a priority when surviving, and setting your priorities straight will definitively bolster your mentality to a winning mindset.

The second part of this skill that you must develop as part of your survival mindset is to always calm down and assess your situation before you develop a strategy and proceed to execute it. Whenever you run into a challenge while surviving outdoors (maybe you failed to capture food for the day or you're encountering great difficulty in starting a fire) always stop what you are doing, take several breaths, assess the situation to identify the problem, formulate a plan to solve the problem, execute the plan, and then re-evaluate how successful the execution was. If you continuously do this throughout each day, you will constantly be both mentally and physically involved in addressing your survival, which will go a long way to reducing panic or a negative mindset.

The next skill to develop is to properly build shelter. Remember that bushcraft is about thriving out in the wilderness, not trying to walk out of it. Therefore, your shelter must be more than a simple shelter that you simply set up to get through the night. In addition, keep in mind that you can only survive for three hours without regulating your body temperature. If it becomes far too sunny or windy outside, shelter is going to be your defense against exposure to those elements. Too many people stuck out in the wilds die of hypothermia or sunstroke, and it kills them in just a matter of hours.

When putting together a shelter, it must be designed to hold up against these kinds of elements, to have enough space for you to live comfortably, be in a strategic location, and provide you with insulation and protection against wind or rain. There are a multitude of different kinds of shelters that you can construct, ranging from simple lean-tos to pits to caves to hollow logs to more complex shelters that you build out of sticks and ropes. As far as location is concerned, your shelter must be near a water source but not directly near it (as protection against flashfloods), facing against the wind, and not exposed out in the open if possible. So for example, if you plan on constructing a large lean to, constructing it deep in the woods rather than at two trees in a field, and a walking distance away from a creek in a direction against the wind would be your best bet.

The next skill that you must learn in bush craft is accumulating, purifying, and storing water. Water is going to be a higher priority than shelter, food, or fire. The ideal amount of water that every individual should drink on a daily basis is one gallon, though you should get by with one half gallon if necessary. You must also divide your water into drinking and cleaning/personal hygiene water, but both types of water must share one thing in common: they should come from the same source, and they should both be cleaned.

The best source for water will be morning dew (can be collected with a rag or bandana), springs, and running streams. Try to avoid still ponds or lakes if you can. Even in running water sources, avoid areas of known chemical contamination (ex. by an agricultural or industrial site), downstream of animal feces or carcasses, at the end of a game trail, or any water that looks muddy. If you fill up your water bottle and it looks dirty, filtering and purifying it isn't going to do much good.

Never drink water directly out of the source. Drinking water that are filled with harmful pathogens and bacteria could end up being more dangerous than not drinking any water at all. There are three ways that you can cleaning out your water, and conducting all three is typically going to be your best bet: filter it in a pump, purify it with iodine tablets, and then boil it for fifteen minutes. If you can do all three of these things to the water you collect, the chances of all of the viruses and bacteria being eliminated will skyrocket. However, some survival experts drink water using only one of those methods, and that works too.

The next skill that you must develop is preparing and maintaining a fire. Otherwise known as Nature's TV, fire does more than just give you something to look at. It gives you security, warmth, light, and a means to cool food. For thousands of years, fire has long been a central survival skill of people. Not only is the mental support it gives you well worth the effort, but you can dry things, cook food, boil your water, get warm at night, and protect yourself against animals.

This is why that you should always keep as many fire starting materials with you as possible. Keep several containers full of matches with you, in addition to several lighters and magnesium flint strikers. Keep a bundle of fire tinder/kindling with you in your pocket as well so you can make fire on the go, and consider keeping Vaseline and cotton balls, candles, or charred cloth with you as well.

But while these amenities are certainly the easiest ways to start fire, you need to start practicing making fire using completely natural resources. The skills you learn to naturally make fire rather than the above devices will be completely invaluable to you. Making fire by friction, such as with the bow drill or the hand drill, are the two most common ways to start a fire naturally. With enough practice, it is possible to start a fire with these methods even when it's pouring down rain. Don't overlook them.

The next skill you must learn is finding food. This means, hunting, fishing, trapping, foraging, and if you're going to be living off the land long enough, cultivating. Food isn't as much of a priority as water, but it's still deeply important and is what keeps your body going. Do research on your local area and find out which plants, greens, or berries will be safe to eat and forage for. Also set traps along trees or game trails with bait to catch small game, and learn how to fish.

Fish in particular are an excellent source of protein, and there are multiple ways to catch them. Rather than using the traditional fishing methods, you can also try spear fishing, hand fishing, net fishing (with large schools of small fish), and setting up a trap where you construct a V shape of stakes in a running stream. When a fish swims into your trap, you close it off and take your prize.

Finally, the last fundamental skill that is an absolute necessity to learn is first aid skills. First Aid is how you act to survive. Accidents and injuries will happen, and not even the slightest of cuts on the tip of a finger can be left unattended. If the injury is more grave, remember to keep your survivalist mentality in action. Do not panic. Breathe, assess your situation, formulate a plan, execute the plan, and then evaluate how the plan worked.

Keep a complete first aid kit with you at all times. Never buy a medical kit that you find in the store; instead, buy all of the contents separately so that you will be one hundred percent familiar with what you have, and consider taking first aid classes where you can get hands on experience and practice. Also keep a knife or hatchet with some rope on hand to cut and tie splints for a sprain or fracture. For both sprain and fractures, the fundamentals are to keep the injured limb elevated with splints (tied off at three different places to keep it the most secured it can be), drink plenty of water with a damp bandana on your head, keep your energy levels up with food, and keep images of your family and loved ones in mind. If it's an open round, tie a tourniquet above it and wrap a bandana over the wound.

Chapter 3: Core Tools for Bushcraft

Maybe you've been stockpiling survival gear for sometime now, so this chapter may not seem so relevant to you. But the more gear you stockpile, the more difficult it will be for you to discover anything that you are missing. The list of tools that you will need for bushcraft may seem a little comprehensive, but it's up to you to decide which ones are the most important to you based on your circumstances or your location.

Every survivalist requires different needs. If you look at the gear load outs of all of the professional survivalists today, you will find that not one has an identical set of gear. Some will be more minimalist while others will be bulkier and more armed to the teeth. You should never be pressured into adopting the same gear load out as anybody else. With that in mind, you should carefully overview the list of survival gear that we will present in this chapter as you select which items you want to include in your load out.

Regardless of what tools and gear you choose to carry for bushcraft, your backpack will be the instrument that holds and organizes your items while you are on the move. Every bushcraft expert would agree that a high quality backpack is an absolute must.

You can either purchase a high quality backpack or you can make one on your own. Many bushcraft experts prefer to make their own backpacks from plant leaves or animal skins. The reasoning behind doing so is because any problems produced from the environment, such as mildew, won't wreck havoc like they would on the fabrics found on backpacks you can buy.

However, this book is about bushcraft for beginners, which means that buying your own backpack from the sporting goods store is going to be the more viable option. If you take care of your backpack by making sure that you keep the fabric dry and sew up any holes that developed, it can last you for years if not decades. When you do buy a backpack, it should be built on an interior aluminum frame, be constructed out of waterproof materials, have several compartments of varying sizes, and receive universally positive reviews from those who have actually used it on the field.

The next tool that most survival experts would consider to be very important is your bushcraft knife, specifically a fixed blade knife. A fixed blade knife will almost always offer more sturdiness than a folding blade, but your knife is still best reserved for light to medium tasks. We're talking things such preparing your food and skinning game, making traps, carving wood, or defending yourself if need be. A good knife can be kept strapped to your side and will always be there when you need it. When looking for a fixed blade knife, look for one where the blade has been built far into the hilt, as these are the most reliable.

Also always consider packing a backup; you never know when you might be glad you had it.

The next important bushcraft tool is a hatchet, and many experts consider the hatchet to be more versatile and thus more useful than your knife. Nonetheless, knives still hold a special place for tasks that are light to medium duty. In contrast, a tomahawk should be best kept for tasks that are heavier duty, such as hammering posts, butchering game, splitting logs, digging into the ground, and chopping wood.

The next tool is a machete, and this is the tool that fills any void between your fixed blade knife and your hatchet. We commonly associate machetes with clearing away brush in thick tropical jungles, but it can also just as easily be used for personal defense, for digging, and for chopping wood or eliminating branches that get in the way. It may not be as handy for lighter duty situations like a knife, but a machete will still definitely get the job done.

In contrast to the knife, hatchet, and machete, the saw is reserved for only one task: to cut down branches. The advantage to owning a saw, nonetheless, is that it is easily the most effective out of all three at this task. Bushcraft is going to require a lot of wood cutting, more than you probably realize, so you'll be glad you have a saw with you when the time comes to make shelter or cut some firewood.

Any of these core bushcraft tools will work well for you for the reasons that we have explained, but you might be asking yourself this: "if I could only have one of these tools, which would it be?" The answer is that every project in bushcraft is going to be made easier with just one of these tools, so the best tool is the one that you have with you.

Our suggestion would be to take as many of these tools with you if you can carry them, but if you can only bring one, than think about what you will be doing most often. If you plan on setting a lot of traps or catching and cleaning fish, take a knife. If you're going to be in some thick brush and need to clear your way through, take a machete. Think before you act, but in due course, you'll find much use for each of these items.

Chapter 4: Becoming Self-Sufficient

Studies show that as many as three quarters of all people want to become self-sufficient, but yet less than five percent will actually attempt to take action to do so. One of the primary reasons why people don't act upon their dreams to become self-sufficient is because they become overwhelmed with fear. Fear is one of the biggest obstacles that people face, because it forces us to focus on the risks rather than the rewards of an endeavor, and only makes us think about the negative consequences of what might happen rather than the positives. For some people, being afraid tells them to be cautious when taking on a new endeavor. But for too many other people, it tells them to be paralyzed and not chase after their dreams at all.

You may be finding yourself in a similar situation. You have too many concerns about self-sustainability that you can't ignore them. But here's the truth: there have been obstacles that you've overcome throughout your entire life.

When you chose your career that you are living now, you certainly faced obstacles in doing so, such as making money to pay for college or getting good grades in college to graduate and get a job. Recall when we talked about developing a survival mentality. You need to take a breath, assess the situation, formulate a plan, execute it, and then evaluate the result.

With that in mind, let's start with taking a breath and assessing the situation. Ask yourself why you want to become self-sustainable, similar to how you asked yourself 'why' when you chose the career you are living now. Asking yourself why you want to become self-sustainable is how you can set the foundation for taking the action to doing so and develop a driving force to push you along. As you ask yourself why you want to become self-sustainable, you'll have to give yourself some answers. Do you seek financial gain or emotional well being? Do you seek an entirely new lifestyle or a sense of adventure?

Ultimately, gaining self-sufficiency is a really simple process. You simply have to make productive habits and drop the habits that set you back. This chapter will teach you new positive habits to gain in regards to self-sustainability and bad habits that you must get rid of.

Starting with the positive habits first…

EMBRACE THE UNKNOWN

You might not know this, but many of the most successful business owners of today actually aren't experts in the business field that they run. All the same, you don't need to be an expert in self-sustainability in order to be successful at it, although knowing as much as you can about it will certainly go a long way to helping. This kind of mindset is what will enable you to embrace the unknown and conquer the fear of living self-sustainably, if that is what is holding you back. If you are afraid of what lies ahead, this will only stifle your future success.

COOK

One of the best ways to make sure that you are eating healthy is to cook food from scratch. That's right, avoid artificial ingredients or preservatives in their entirety, in addition to foods that have been processed and/or pre-cooked. To cook from scratch, you'll just need to give it a go. Trial and error process is one of the most effective ways that we learn to become good at anything, and the same holds true for cooking.

For the outdoors, the best type of cookware that you can use to cook will be cast iron materials. These kinds of materials hold up well over an outdoor fire, so you can take them out and practice cooking over an open fire perhaps even in your own backyard.

While we have touched based on this previously in this book, learning to make a few is an absolute necessity for bushcraft. Cooking is certainly going to be a major challenge, if not an impossibility, without knowing how to start a fire. Therefore, it would make sense that you practice as several different ways to build a fire as you can in a manner that you aren't limited to certain resources or conditions. Fire building and cooking are two skills that go hand in hand with self-sustainability.

As soon as you've gotten fire making and cooking down, you can then try your hand at your other cooking skills such as adding seasoning or trying something different with your game. Eventually, your confidence in your cooking abilities will grow the point that you'll be able to make any meal in any situation.

GARDENING

Learning to garden is arguably the toughest habit to develop of the ones in this chapter, and indeed, it will prove a challenge if you don't have a lot of land that you can cultivate. Nonetheless, many gardening and survival experts alike are able to make much out of little. Methods such as companion planting (where you group plants that complement each other closely together) are commonly used by people who live in urban areas or have limited land available to them.

Regardless of whether you plan on cultivating vast acres or just a few pots by the windowsill, the basics of gardening remain the same. The heart and soul of any garden is the seeds. Stick with heirloom seeds and stock up on them in storage so that you'll never run out. Always store your seeds in cooler rooms and away from the sun. The seeds should be ones that will grow well in your particular environment or climate, so do your research.

At the very end of each growing season, you will want to compost foliage to ensure that you have a healthy supply of soil rich in nutrients for the harvest in the next year. Rainwater is a gift from the heavens, so never let any of it go to waste. Keep barrels and construct rain catchments systems outside to catch all of the rainwater that falls, and then save that water for your garden when the days are hot and the rain is scarce.

Some plants will be able to pollinate by themselves, but most others will require the aid of the gardener in order to pollinate. Once your vegetable has reached the full color and size, you can proceed to harvest it. Don't be disheartened if your first harvest doesn't exactly go as planned and you find that pests have destroyed some of your crops. Gardening is a trial and error process where you will improve your skills with each new harvest.

Eventually, you might even get to the point where you produce a greater harvest than you can possible consume. If this happens, then learning good preservation skills will certainly come in handy. No bushcraft expert allows any food to go to waste. You can easily can the majority of fruits and vegetables to be stored safely for later.

BE THRIFTY

Adopting a thrifty lifestyle will go a very long ways towards successfully living self-sufficiently. Being thrifty will require you to take a good look at how much you are spending and any ways that you can cut back. Adopting thrifty habits with your finances will enable you to better transition over to adopting similar thrifty habits out in the wilds.

There are numerous ways that you will be able to cut any waste of resources or spending that you making and make little resources go much further. Just a few examples of what you can do is to make your own materials. For instance, you can easily make your own soaps out of some plants. You can also purchase foods in bulk for a better deal, and get rid of any extra items that you have at garage sales.

You can also develop hobbies that are more productive. Spending your time playing video games is an example of a hobby that is not productive, but learning to repair cars or furniture, developing better cooking skills, hiking, or reading are all examples of hobbies that are productive. Learning to repair things means that you'll become more resourceful not only for yourself, but also for those you know. Developing better cooking skills means you can learn to cook better and perhaps with more limited resources, while hiking can give you a physical workout and also enhance your mental well-being as you enjoy nature. Finally, reading also increases your knowledge of the world around you.

Taking control of your finances and developing productive hobbies are often times the first steps you can take to living a more thrifty lifestyle. When you're on your own in the wilderness with extremely limited resources, you will be less overwhelmed by having to make much out of what little you have.

However, there are also bad habits that you will want to get rid of. Every person on this planet has good habits, but everyone also has bad habits that could range from negativity to addictions to limited activities. Let's discuss some bad habits that you will need to get rid of, as they can impede your ability to become self-sufficient.

The first bad habit is an addiction. Having a strong dependence on a substance will severely impede your self-sufficiency efforts since your mind will constantly be clouded by your emotional and perhaps even physical desire to have whatever it is you are addicted to. Not only that, but addictions often will be detrimental to our physical health and lower our lifespan significantly.

Many people believe that in order to give up on an addiction they have to give up on it overnight. This is simply an impossible task. Instead, cut back progressively on whatever you are addicted to until you feel comfortable releasing yourself from it entirely, even if this process takes several months. Being open and receiving support from friends and family members always helps as well.

The next bad addiction is having a poor diet. Just like how your car needs gasoline to fuel itself, you need food and water to fuel yourself. But if you put the wrong type of gasoline into your car, it's definitely not going to run good. The same holds true for your eating habits. Eating too much foods or not getting enough nutrition will greatly impact you negatively. Next time you go grocery shopping, look for foods that are high in nutrition. If you overeat, treat it like an addiction and progressively cut back on how much you eat each day, but don't get to where you eat too little that you feel sick.

The next big negative habit is constantly feeling negative about yourself. When you fail to accomplish a goal, you beat yourself up too hard, but when you do accomplish something, you don't give yourself enough gratitude. Take a breath and express gratitude toward yourself consistently throughout the day to create positive thinking. In addition, if you fail to accomplish a goal, reassess what you did wrong and then correct the problem based on that assessment rather than beating yourself up needlessly.

The final negative habit that we will discuss is getting low physical activity. This is a habit that many people in our society today are dealing with, by sitting for too long in front of the TV or the computer. We're not saying that you have to banish yourself from these technological outlets, but we are saying that if you struggle with low physical activity levels, that you will need to balance the amount of time you spend on these devices with the amount of time that you spend outside.

Becoming self-sufficient will require great endurance and dedication on your part, but the good news is that once you do become self-sufficient, you will be much better prepared for making it out of any survival situation and will no longer be dependent on outside sources.

Chapter 5: Bushcraft Projects for Beginners

Sooner or later, you're going to need to take the knowledge that you have learned in this book and convert that into the skills to survive. If you're nervous about doing so, that's understandable. But you should never be afraid about beginning to test out your skills. Keep in mind, there was a time where the most professional bushcraft survival experts today hadn't tested out their own skills.

To give you a head start to put your bushcraft skills in action, we've put together directions for three bushcraft projects that beginners can try at home.

PROJECT #1 - SLING SHOT PROJECT

Would you feel comfortable using a sling shot as a hunting tool or weapon? You might not, since the last time you probably used one was while playing with your friends as a child. However, a sling shot can actually be a formidable weapon, and making your own sling shot will only further your confidence in the weapon.

We're not saying that a sling shot should your first choice for a hunting tool or weapon, but it certainly is an option to consider. Plus, building your own be a fun process that will increase your confidence in yourself as a survivalist. Some of the top bushcraft experts have been known to take down big game with slingshots and put food on the table for weeks if not months.

To make an effective sling shot, you'll need a tree branch in the shape of a Y, strips of leather, surgical tubing, dental floss, a knife, a saw, and at least an hour of your time.

The first step is to find a work in the tree. The branch must be shaped like a Y, and preferably be oak, hickory, or hard maple wood. These kinds of woods are fairly easy to find and will be strong enough for your slingshot. The Y-shape doesn't have to be perfect, since finding a perfectly shaped Y branch is going to take up a lot of your time. Look for a thirty degree angle at best.

After you've found your branch and cut it away, you can now begin to dry out the wood. Since you've just cut your branch from the tree, chances are that it's going to have a lot of moisture left in it. This gives it too much flexibility and isn't going to be good for an effective sling shot. You need a slingshot that won't break. Start a campfire and set your branch by the flames, not close enough so that it will burn, but not too far so that the moisture won't be sucked out. If you have access to a microwave at home, that will work well too.

Next, take your medical tubing. You're going to have to use your own discretion for how long the tubing should be based on the size of the branch. If the tubing is too short, you won't be able to pull it back, but if it's too long, the power of the rock or stone being shot won't be as high.

After finding your desired length, cut the tubing into two equal sizes.

One end of the tubing should be tied around the notch until it doubles back. The end of the tube should be tied to the other end with dental floss. If there are any long ends hanging after it is tied, cut them off.

You should easily be able to find leather at a local store. Cut it into a 4x2 rectangle, with two holds at each of the long ends through which you can attach the tubing. From then on, slide the tubing through the leather holes, and then folds the ends of the tubes with dental floss.

PROJECT #2 - DRINKING STRAW SEWING KIT

For this project, you will need thread and a needle, electrical tape, a safety pin, and a few drinking straws. You should plan on making multiple drinking straw sewing kits as no single one is going to fulfill all of the roles that you need them for.

Take the needle and then thread it with several feet of thread. You can then tie a not onto the end of it, pulling it towards the needles eye. Next, take your safety pin and insert it over an inch into the straw's end. Fold it over and then close it off with the electrical tape. There are other options for sealing it off, but electrical tape is our first recommendation.

Next, proceed to fit all of this into your drinking straw. Take both ends of the straw, bend them, and then tape or tie them off. To wrap it up (literally), take more electrical tape and then wrap it around the straw for extra durability.

The drinking straw sewing kits are extremely narrow, lightweight, and can be stored practically anywhere. Due to the ease and simplicity of putting one together, you can also construct several of them for different purposes and store them in different locations. The thread and needle can then be removed and used to repair clothing and equipment alike while on the go.

PROJECT #3 – Firebow

Earlier in this book, we discussed the importance of building fires. While using easy amenities such as a lighter, magnesium flint striker, or a match will always come in handy, you must always be prepared to make a fire when these things aren't available to you. For this scenario, the firebow method is going to be the most effective. We're about to teach you how you can start a fire with this method, but as a reminder, you have to do more than just read the directions. Practice it extensively until you've mastered the art.

The first object that you will need is a wooden board. This is known as the fireboard. If you go with a branch for your fireboard, split it evenly down the middle until it is as thick as your thumb. Eliminate any part of the wood that protrudes out.

Next, you'll need to make the spindle. The spindle can be made with a foot long piece of wood that is whittled down into an inch in diameter. Each end will then need to be sharpened.

The next piece is the handhold, which can be made by taking a branch that is sawed into a five inch long piece. Any parts of the wood that protrude out should be thoroughly eliminated so you can get a solid grip on the wood. Next, on the flat side of the handhold, take your knife or hatchet and cut a half inch hole in the center. The end of the hole should slope at a roughly forty five degree angle.

The next piece you'll need is cordage, and simple paracord should work nicely. The string should be at least one quarter thick and almost twice as long as the bow. Many people try to use shoelaces to fulfill the rule of the cordage, but most will not fit either of the requirements. If you don't have any cordage with you, you can always try using vine.

Next, you'll need to make the centerpiece of the project: the actual bow. Find a green branch that is as thick as your index finger and as long as your forearm. The bow can never be flimsy, but it should be flexible enough so that it can be slightly bent into a curved shape. Make sure that the bow is flexible throughout and doesn't have any weak points.

Once you have accumulated these materials, all of which can be gained naturally in the wilderness, you can now go about the process of starting your fire. Take your knife or hatchet and split two inches into the wood on both ends of the bow. The fact that the branch must be green comes into play here, and splitting a drier piece of wood would cause it to perhaps split all the way down, forcing you to start all the way over. Set your bow down on the wood board so that the splits are parallel to the surface.

Next, take your cordage and tie them in the splits with a firm knot. Make sure that this is repeated with both ends of the bow. Take your splindle, and wrap the cord around it in the middle. When tying both ends of the cord to the bow, you want to make sure that there's enough flexibility in the cord so that there's enough to wrap it around the spindle.

You can now begin to make the hole in the handhold. Keeping pressure on the handhold, use your bow and spindle to make the hole by running the bow back and forth until smoke begins to appear on either the end of the spindle or the handhold. Blow way any dust that appears but pick up the speed once it starts to smoke. Continue this process until the handhold hole is the same diameter as your spindle. The point of drilling this hole in the handhold is so that the spindle will not slip out and derail your attempt to start the fire.

Next, repeat this process by drilling a hole into the fireboard. Again, you want smoke to appear on the spindle and the board and you should wipe away any dust that appears. Remember to use the entire cordage on the bow as you move the spindle.

After you've drilled the holes, cut a notch with your knife or hatchet by the resulting socket. The notch should be triangular in shape, and this is where the coal will form together on the tinder. If the notch is too big, the spindle will easily fly out and you'll have to start over. But if the notch is too small, then it won't get enough oxygen to start a spark. Place a sheet of bark or paper underneath the notch so that it can catch any coals that fall out.

Next, collect some tinder and clump it together. When you begin to drill and produce smoker, make sure that the tinder is held close to the coals so that a flame can catch when you blow into it.

After this, you can then work the firebow into the fireboard hold and notch just like you were doing before. The spindle should be held firmly in the holes of the handhold and the fireboard. Keep one food on the fireboard to hold it stead, your dominant hand working the firebow, and then your other hand on the handhold. This part will take a lot of practice, and you will likely fail on your first few attempts. You may have to drill new holes and cut new notches later on. But as long as you keep your back straight and don't give up, you will eventually produce smoke and your tinder will catch a flame from the coals. Each time you work at it, the easier it will be and less amount of time consuming it will be.

Try practicing the firebow method over weekends. Once you get the hang of it, performing the action out in the woods won't seem like such a big deal.

Conclusion

Congratulations! You have now learned the fundamentals you will need for thriving in and being fully self-sustainable out in the wilderness. Far too many individuals in this day and age are disconnected from nature and too dependent on the technology that they have been accustomed too. Subsequently, should they ever find themselves in a survival situation, they're definitely going to face a seemingly impossible challenge.

Thousands of years ago, are ancestors didn't just learn to make it out of the wilderness. They learned to live in it and be fully self-sustainable. All the same, you can learn to thrive in the wilderness even in this day and age. There are an abundance of sources, both textual and online, that you can find for learning to make it out of a survival situation. But there are far too few resources dedicated to true bushcraft: learning to flourish out in the wilderness with the bare necessities instead of just trying to make it back to civilization.

By learning to be totally self-sustainable out in the wilderness, you will have cultivated for yourself an invaluable life skill. If you ever find yourself lost out in the wilds, you'll be at peace and in harmony with nature rather than panicky and desperate to make your way out. In essence, you'll be just like how your ancestors were thousands of years before you, and be a major step or two ahead of those you know who are too connected to the technological equipment they have become accustomed to.

Throughout this book, you have learned what true bushcraft really is, the foundational survival skills that you will keep with you for the rest of your life, the tools you need, how to become truly self-sustainable in the wilderness, and then projects that you can initiate at home to begin converting your knowledge into skills.

Is this book the only resource you should read up on bushcraft? Absolutely not. But there is no better source you have found that has taught you the basics of bushcraft condensed into this little of space. The knowledge that you have learned in this book will serve as the foundation for what the rest of your knowledge and skills is based off of for the rest of your life. That's an invaluable set of knowledge that so many other people don't have the luxury of learning.

Good luck!